IN FOCUS

OCEANS AND SEAS

KINGFISHER
LONDON & NEW YORK

Copyright © Macmillan Publishers International Ltd 2017
Published in the United States by Kingfisher,
175 Fifth Ave., New York, NY 10010
Kingfisher is an imprint of Macmillan Children's Books, London
All rights reserved.

Distributed in the U.S. and Canada by Macmillan,
175 Fifth Ave., New York, NY 10010

Library of Congress Cataloging-in-Publication data has been applied for.

Series editor: Hayley Down
Designer: Jeni Child

ISBN (PB): 978-0-7534-7348-1
ISBN (HB): 978-0-7534-7347-4

Kingfisher books are available for special promotions
and premiums. For details contact: Special Markets
Department, Macmillan, 175 Fifth Ave.,
New York, NY 10010.

For more information, please visit
www.kingfisherbooks.com

Printed in China

9 8 7 6 5 4 3 2 1

1TR/0417/WKT/UG/128MA

IN FOCUS

OCEANS AND SEAS

BY STEVE PARKER

KINGFISHER
NEW YORK

© Disney/Pixar

CONTENTS

WATER WORLD

Arctic Ocean

Atlantic Ocean

Pacific Ocean

Atlantic Ocean

Southern Ocean

EARTH'S SURFACE

FAST FACT

is covered by . . .

Seas and oceans:
136 million sq. mi.
(352 million km²)

Land: 5.95 million sq. mi.
(149 million km²)

Our planet is called "Earth," but maybe it should be called "Ocean"! More than two-thirds of its surface is covered by the salty water of oceans and seas. That's twice as much as all of the land and the fresh (nonsalty) water of rivers and lakes. Seas and oceans are the biggest, deepest, and most exciting places in the world. Let's explore them!

% OF WATER ON EARTH:

Seas and oceans: 96.5
Ice caps, glaciers, and snow: 1.7
Under the ground: 1.6
Lakes and rivers: less than 0.2

Arctic Ocean

Pacific Ocean

Indian Ocean

Southern Ocean

PLANET OCEAN

FAMOUS FIVE

Earth may look like it has one giant ocean, but we have divided it into five parts—each with different features!

ARCTIC OCEAN

Area: 6.2 million sq. mi. (16 million km²)
% of Earth's surface covered: 3
Average depth: 3,955 ft. (1,206 m)
Greatest depth: 18,439 ft. (5,620 m)
The Arctic is the smallest, shallowest, and coldest ocean. In the winter, it is mostly covered in floating sheets of ice. Even in the summer there is floating ice in the middle, at the North Pole.

ATLANTIC OCEAN

Area: 33 million sq. mi. (85 million km²)
% of Earth's surface covered: 17
Average depth: 12,875 ft. (3,925 m)
Greatest depth: 30,250 ft. (9,220 m)
The Atlantic has huge waves and fierce **hurricanes**. Much of its coastline is rocky with tall cliffs. It is divided into two almost equal parts: the North and South Atlantic Oceans.

INDIAN OCEAN

Area: 27 million sq. mi. (70 million km²)
% of Earth's surface covered: 14
Average depth: 12,990 ft. (3,960 m)
Greatest depth: 24,460 ft. (7,455 m)
The Indian Ocean is the warmest, with many large and small islands and beautiful coral reefs. It is usually calm, except for monsoon storms that bring rain to South Asia from July to September.

PACIFIC OCEAN

Area: 65 million sq. mi. (169 million km²)
% of Earth's surface covered: 33
Average depth: 13,222 ft. (4,030 m)
Greatest depth; 36,200 ft. (11,033 m)
The widest ocean, the Pacific covers almost one-third of Earth. It has more than 20,000 islands. Some have no people and almost no animals—except for a few seabirds!

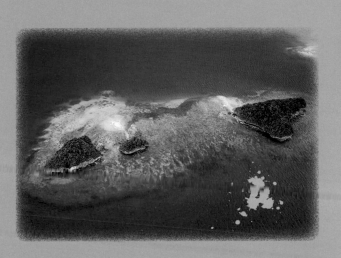

SOUTHERN OCEAN

Area: 8.5 million sq. mi. (22 million km²)
% of Earth's surface covered: 4
Average depth: 14,756 sq. mi (4500 m)
Greatest depth: 23,735 sq. mi. (7235 m)
Wild and stormy in the winter, the Southern Ocean has the strongest average winds on Earth. It has many huge icebergs that break free from the great ice-covered landmass of Antarctica.

GO WITH THE FLOW

Oceans and seas are never still. Even when the surface looks calm, water is moving beneath, as flowing currents. These vary from a small, gentle drift along the shore to gigantic torrents as millions of tons of water rush through the deep ocean faster than you can run!

Riding currents:

Animals that travel long distances swim with currents to help speed their journeys. Blue sharks cross the North Atlantic with the Gulf Stream to reach Europe, and then head south to ride the North Equatorial Current back to North America.

WAVES
AND
TIDES

Your questions about waves answered, including what makes them!

What is a tsunami?

A tsunami is caused by an **earthquake** under the ocean. The shifting seabed makes a massive ripple of water that travels hundreds of miles. When it reaches land, it surges ashore as a giant wave, causing terrible damage.

How are waves made?

Far out in the ocean, wind heaps up large ridges of water called swells. As the swells move toward the shore, water piles up above the shallow seabed into tall waves that topple over, or break, and crash roaring white foam onto the land.

How do tides happen?

Tides are due to the **gravity**, or pull, of the Moon and the Sun. Gravity pulls Earth's water nearest the Moon or Sun into a bulge, making a high tide! As Earth spins each day, the bulges travel around it, about once every 12½ hours.

Why do some places have big tides and others almost none?

Where currents and tidal waters flow into a narrow area between land on each side, the tidal range (the difference between high and low tides) is greater. On straight, open coasts the range is smaller. Try pouring the same amount of water into a bowl and a glass—the water will be higher in the glass because there is less room to spread out.

TOP 10

OCEAN WONDERS

Far below the waves are some of Earth's biggest, most spectacular sights—if you have a submarine!

Mid-Atlantic Ridge

At 9,940 mi. (16,000 km) long, this split in the middle of the Atlantic is the world's longest **mountain range**. This diver is exploring a **fissure** called the Silfra Crack.

2 North Pole

The North Pole is under drifting ice sheets in the Arctic Ocean. If you plant a flag on the ice above the North Pole, it will float away.

7 Monterey Canyon

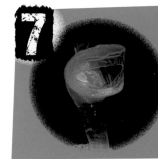

This canyon is near California. At 93 mi (150 km) long, it is similar to the Grand Canyon and is home to strange deep-sea animals!

3 Tristan da Cunha

In the South Atlantic, 1,300 mi. (2,400 km) from mainland Africa, this tiny place is Earth's most isolated island.

8 Cape Horn

Fierce storms blow at the tip of South America, where the Pacific and Atlantic Oceans meet. Winds there rage at more than 62 mph (100 km/h).

4 Mauna Kea

This Hawaiian peak is the tallest **seamount**. At 32,800 ft, (10,000 m) tall, it's taller than Mount Everest!

9 Waterspouts

The Florida Keys is a great place to spot these twisting funnels of water spray. Similar to **tornadoes**, some reach more than 3,280 ft (1000 m) into the sky!

5 Bay of Fundy

The world's biggest tides are on Canada's east coast. The water flows into a narrow inlet, creating tides of more than 52 ft. (16 m)!

10 Mariana Trench

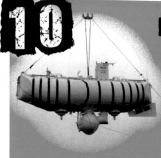

In the Western Pacific is the deepest place on Earth: 7 mi. (11 km) below sea level. Only two crewed vessels have been there, in 1960 (pictured) and 2012.

6 Maelstrom of Saltstraumen

Near Norway, currents and tides combine as whirlpools called maelstroms, swirling at 30 mph (50 km/h)!

Which wonder would you like to explore?

SUPER SEAS!

A sea is a very large area of water that is partly surrounded by land, usually at the edge of an ocean. There are more than 100 seas on Earth!

FAST FACT

CARIBBEAN SEA

Area: 1.06 million sq. mi. (2.75 million km²)
Average depth: 7,200 ft. (2,200 m)
The Caribbean Sea is one of the warmest seas, with many coral reefs and a string of tropical islands to the north and the east.

NORTH SEA

FAST FACT

Area: 0.22 million sq. mi. (0.57 million km²)
Average depth: 300 ft. (95 m)
The shallow, stormy North Sea is busy with ships, oil rigs, and wind farms that produce clean energy!

FAST FACT

MEDITERRANEAN SEA

Area: 1 million sq. mi. (2.5 million km²)
Average depth: 5,000 ft. (1,500 m)
The Mediterranean Sea is mostly warm and calm. Nicknamed the "Med," it has busy vacation resorts around its beautiful beaches.

SOUTH CHINA SEA

Area: 1.4 million sq. mi. (3.5 million km²)
Average depth: 8,500 ft. (2,600 m)
Thousands of ships crisscross this sea carrying goods or tourists between the islands.

RED SEA

Area: 0.17 million sq. mi. (0.44 million km²)
Average depth: 1,590 ft. (485 m)
Teeming with tropical fish and other creatures, the Red Sea is very warm, rarely rough, and is surrounded by deserts.

CORAL SEA

Area: 1.9 million sq. mi.
(4.8 million km²)
Average depth: 7,900 ft. (2,400 m)
Although usually sunny, the Coral Sea can be whipped up by cyclones. The Great Barrier Reef is found here.

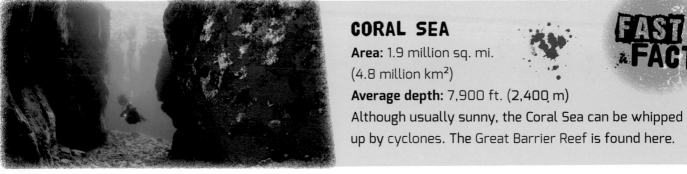

WEDDELL SEA

Area: 1.1 million sq. mi. (2.8 million km²)
Average depth: 7,550 ft. (2,300 m)
Like a huge bay partly enclosed by Antarctica, the Weddell Sea is frozen over in the winter and crowded with icebergs the rest of the year.

OCEAN EDGES

Ocean and land constantly battle each other! When a river erodes (wears away) its banks, **shingle**, sand, and mud are made and washed into the sea, where flat areas of land known as **bars** and **spits** may form. When a volcano erupts and its hot, runny **lava** flows into the water, the lava can cool into a solid rock island. In other places, the ocean wins, as great storms, crashing waves, and powerful currents erode the land.

FAST FACT

Tall, dark **CLIFFS** are made of hard rock, usually granite or basalt. The waves wear away or undercut the base to leave an overhang, which eventually tumbles into the sea. White cliffs are usually made of chalk rock, which is soft.

overhang
cliff

mangroves

FAST FACT

In **TROPICAL AREAS** where tides, waves, and currents are gentle, mud collects along the shore and mangrove trees can grow. Where currents and tides are stronger, long, sandy beaches form.

iceberg

FAST FACT

CURRENTS, WINDS, WAVES, and **TIDES** wear rocks or ice into amazing shapes, such as caves, arches, and tall, upright columns called stacks. A big storm may tear them down in seconds.

salt pan

FAST FACT

In flat, shallow areas, water can **EVAPORATE** (dry up) to reveal salt pans. These are areas of land covered by glistening sea salt left behind by the water.

OCEAN LIFE

HOME SWEET HOME

Your questions about wonderful ocean habitats answered!

Which habitats are between land and sea?

Coastal habitats vary from smooth mudflats to steep cliffs. Along the **low tide mark** and in the **shallows** are many kinds of seaweeds. They are home to crabs, shellfish, and animals that feed on them, such as sea otters!

Where does most ocean wildlife live?

Living things thrive in calm, shallow, sunlit waters—especially in the **tropics**! Some animals here have bright colors, but others blend in with their background; this is called **camouflage**. In some places, coral reefs grow.

What's the biggest habitat in the world?

The open ocean covers more than half of Earth, and most of it is more than 10,000 ft. (3,000 m) deep. This is the realm of the world's biggest, fastest, fiercest predators, such as sharks, swordfish, and orcas. It is also home to the world's most massive beasts: whales!

Where is it always dark and almost freezing?

Vast areas of the deep ocean bed are flat plains covered with muddy ooze. There is no light or warmth from the sun, so it is dark and cold all the time. Strange fish, worms, shrimp, crabs, sponges, and starfish have adapted to this never-changing habitat.

ALONG THE SHORE

Shores are tough places to live! Plants and animals endure hot sun, drying winds, soaking rain, roaring waves, swishing currents, and the constant rise and fall of the tide. Muddy and sandy shores may look empty when the tide is out, but many creatures are hiding beneath the surface.

As the tide rises, animals come out to search for food. Rocky coasts have big boulders and sheltered rock pools, teeming with fish and other animals. But the stones on shingle and pebble beaches are rolled around by the waves, making it hard for living things to survive on these shores.

FAST FACT

SEA TURTLES come to sandy beaches to lay their eggs. The female digs a pit with her flippers, lays eggs in the bottom, covers them with sand, and then lumbers slowly back to the sea . . .

turtle hatchling

. . . Months later, **TURTLE** hatchlings crack out of their eggs and dig their way to the surface. They race to the sea as fast as possible to avoid being eaten by predators on the way.

anemone

They look like flowers, but **ANEMONES** are animals—and they're hungry! They catch prey, such as fish and shrimp, in their stinging tentacles and pass it into their mouth in the center of their body.

FAST FACT

The **COCONUT CRAB** is big and strong. It can live out of water for hours or even days. It eats almost anything, from seeds and leaves to rotting plants or old meat. It also climbs trees!

coconut crab

mudskipper

MUDSKIPPERS dig a burrow where they hide from enemies. They can jump and skip very fast using their front fins and tail, as they hunt for small worms, shellfish, and other prey.

FAST FACT

CORAL WONDERLAND

Coral reefs cover less than 1 percent of all the oceans' area, yet they are home to 25 percent of ocean animals. Reefs are made of small, simple animals called coral polyps. Polyps build stony cases around themselves. As they die and more polyps grow, the cases build up into the reef's beautiful shapes.

The Great Barrier Reef:

Off the coast of northeast Australia, the Great Barrier Reef is Earth's biggest coral reef. It is almost 1,430 mi. (2,300 km) long and 30–155 mi. (50–250 km) wide. It is home to over 600 kinds of coral, 3,000 different shellfish, and 1,600 types of fish!

SEA ANEMONES are named after the anemone flower on land because their tentacles look like petals.

CORAL REEFS

Find out the facts about the reef's most fascinating inhabitants!

The **CLOWN FISH** has a special, slimy body covering that protects it from an anemone's stings. The fish keeps the anemone clean by eating scraps of its leftover food.

CLEANER SHRIMP walk gently over larger fish and other animals to pick off old scales, skin pests, and other small bits. This helps the bigger creature stay clean—and the shrimp gets a meal!

Long, sharp, stinging spines make some **STARFISH** dangerous reef dwellers. The big crown-of-thorns starfish is especially venomous and damages reefs by eating coral polyps.

POWDER BLUE TANGS grow to 10 in. (25 cm) long. A sharp spine at the base of their tail protects them against enemies.

Lurking in a cave or crack, the **MORAY EEL** can dart its head out and bite in a flash.

The **GIANT GROUPER** is more than 8 ft. (2.5 m) long and weighs over 770 lb. (350 kg). It lies in wait among the coral and is so massive that it can swallow a small turtle or baby shark in one gulp!

The **BLACKTIP REEF SHARK** grabs any prey it can, including fish, squid, crabs, seabirds, and even young seals!

Up to 3 ft. (1 m) across, the **GIANT CLAM** weighs as much as three adult humans! It sucks in water to filter out pieces of food, and closes its shell against enemies.

A **SEA HORSE** sucks food through its tubelike mouth. Its tail holds on to seaweed or coral.

SPECTACULAR

PELICAN

The brown pelican flaps slowly above the sea, spots a fish, and dives at speed into the water. After grabbing the fish, it pushes most of the water out of its balloonlike throat pouch before gulping down the meal.

brown pelican

STORM PETREL

The storm petrel is tiny—hardly the size of a garden sparrow. Yet, except for during **breeding** time, it spends almost every minute in the air. Its main food is small fish and similar creatures. It picks them from the water's surface as it swoops down, or "patters" by running along the surface.

storm petrel

sea eagle

puffins

SEABIRDS

Oceans are a great source of food for seabirds. These birds can be as small as your hand or as long as an adult human!

ALBATROSS

The wandering albatross has the longest wings of any bird! Each wing is as long as an adult person is tall! This huge bird glides for hours without flapping and stays airborne for a year or more. It skims low over the waves to grab small fish and squid.

albatross

GANNET

When it spies a fish below, the northern gannet folds back its wings and dives like a feathery arrow. It hits the water at 62 mph (100 km/h)—as fast as a car on the interstate! It flaps its strong, webbed feet to chase prey that swims as deep as 65 ft. (20 m) below the water's surface.

gannet

TOP 10

OCEAN CHAMPIONS

There are many record-breaking ocean creatures, including the biggest, longest, fastest, and most numerous—and don't forget the floppiest!

1 Blue whale

The biggest creature ever to live on Earth, the blue whale can be 100 ft. (30 m) long and weigh over 175 tons. It eats 4.5 tons of food every day!

2. Leatherback turtle

At 1,550 lb. (700 kg) in weight and 13 ft. (4 m) across, this is the biggest turtle. It eats mostly jellyfish!

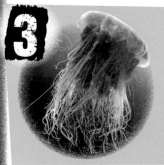

3. Lion's mane jellyfish

The body of the lion's mane reaches 8 ft. (2.5 m) across. Its stinging tentacles trail for 100 ft. (30 m) or more.

4. Whale shark

Weighing 22 tons, the biggest fish is the whale shark. It swims with its huge mouth open to catch krill!

5. Krill

Small cousins of shrimp and prawns, krill are among the world's most numerous creatures. They are the main food for fish, squid, and even great whales!

6. Saltwater crocodile

Biggest of all reptiles, the aggressive "saltie" grows to 23 ft. (7 m) and weighs more than a ton.

7. Sailfish

Fastest in the sea, the sailfish folds its top fin along its back. At 68 mph (110 km/h), it's almost as fast as a cheetah is on land!

8. Super squid

Huge jumbo squid, and even bigger giant and colossal squid, prowl the ocean. They are the largest invertebrates (animals without a backbone).

9. Oarfish

Like a sea serpent of stories and legends, the oarfish is the longest bony fish. It can stretch for 36 ft. (11 m)—more than the longest snake, the python.

10. Sunfish

This is the heaviest fish with a bony **skeleton**. Weighing more than 2.2 tons, it reaches 15 ft. (4.5 m) in length, and the same in height.

Which record breaker is your number one?

FREEZING OCEANS

Salty seawater doesn't freeze until it reaches minus 28°F (– 2°C). Some animals can cope with the near-freezing polar waters—although they do so in different ways!

FAST FACT

Warm-blooded sea animals, such as whales, have a thick, jellylike layer of fatty **BLUBBER** under their skin. This works like a coat to keep in body heat. The bowhead whale has blubber more than 20 in. (50 cm) thick!

bowhead whale

WHAT'S THE TEMPERATURE?

Home bath: **102–104°F (39–40°C)**
Warmest sea water: **95°F (35°C)**
Tropical coral reef: **86°F (30°C)**

Cold tap at home: **45–50°F (7–10°C)**
Bottom of the deep sea: **36–37°F (2–3°C)**
Coldest sea water: **28°F (–2°C)**

icefish

Cold-blooded **FISH** are usually the same temperature as the water around them. Polar fish, such as icefish, have chemicals in their blood to keep them from freezing solid.

SLEEPER SHARKS are huge and old. The Greenland sleeper reaches more than 20 ft. (6 m) in length and lives for over 350 years! They are called "sleepers" because they stay still in the icy water for long periods.

Greenland sleeper

rockhopper penguins

PENGUINS have layers of feathers to keep warm. They include long, strong feathers on the outside and two kinds of short, fluffy feathers underneath. A penguin is a cozy 100.4°F (38°C) inside—a bit warmer than you!

MEET THE MAMMALS!

The main groups of sea mammals are cetaceans, such as dolphins and whales; pinnipeds, such as sealions, walrus and seals; and sirenians, such as dugongs and manatees.

The **DALL'S PORPOISE** looks like a mini killer whale. It prefers cool northern waters where it dives down 330 ft. (100 m) or more to feed on fish and squid.

Slim and fast, the 10 ft. (3 m)–long **LEOPARD SEAL** prowls the Southern Ocean around Antarctica. Its favorite food is penguins— although it spits out the feathers!

DUGONGS live around the coasts of the Indian and West Pacific Oceans. They are called "sea cows" because they spend hours feeding on seagrass plants.

As the second-biggest animal in the world, the **FIN WHALE** is slim, sleek, and speedy. It reaches a speed of 30 mph (50 km/h)—faster than the quickest human runner!

The smallest sea mammal is not from one of the main groups; it's the **SEA OTTER** of North American coasts. It weighs just 65 lb. (30 kg).

Thousands of **COMMON DOLPHINS** gather in groups, called pods. These dolphins often leap in the air.

At more than 4.5 tons, the massive male **ELEPHANT SEAL** weighs as much as an elephant!

TOP 10

DEADLY ANIMALS

These animals can be dangerous to people—and some are truly deadly!

1 Great white shark

The great white shark carries out some of the 50–100 shark attacks each year—but usually fewer than 10 people die.

2

Blue-ringed octopus

Beware this octopus if its rings glow blue! This means it may bite, and its bite can kill!

7

Stonefish

Lying on a weedy rock, the stonefish is so well camouflaged that it is easy to step on. The spines on its back jab in a strong venom that can cause death.

3

Barracuda

If a great barracuda comes near humans, it's usually just curious. But a sudden movement can cause it to bite with needle-sharp teeth.

8

Sea snake

Sea snakes spend all their life at sea. Their venom can kill a human, but they usually use it to kill fish.

4

Crown-of-thorns starfish

This big, spiny starfish has extremely powerful venom that causes pain, bleeding, and swelling.

9

Cone shell

This sea snail may look slow and harmless. But a quick jab from its short, sharp, dart-like spine causes extreme pain— and can even be fatal.

5

Stingray

Lying peacefully on the seabed, the stingray may strike if suddenly disturbed. Its daggerlike sting is on the underside of its tail.

10

Bull shark

Bull sharks are smaller than great whites, but more aggressive! Attacks blamed on great whites are often by bull sharks.

6

Sea wasp (box jellyfish)

At 12 in. (30 cm) across, with long, trailing tentacles, the sea wasp can cause one of the world's most painful stings!

Which deadly animal is the most terrifying?

CLOSE UP

OCEAN WANDERER

About 3 ft. (1 m) long, loggerheads are medium-sized sea turtles. They live in the warm waters of the Atlantic and Pacific. Each year, they swim with currents to find their favorite foods. Some of them cross the entire Pacific Ocean, between the east coast of East Asia and the west coast of North America, and then back again.

More about loggerheads:

Length: 20 in. (90 cm)
Average lifespan: 50 years
Food: Crabs, conchs, and jellyfish
Female loggerheads return to the beach
where they hatched to lay their own eggs.

KILLER WHALES

Your questions about killer whales answered—including why they are also called orcas!

Why do we call them "orcas?"

The nickname "orca" comes from an ancient Roman god of the underworld, Orcus. Orcas are also nicknamed "blackfish" because of their skin. Of course, orcas are not fish at all—they are mammals! Orcas are not whales either—they are really the biggest kind of dolphin!

killer whale hunting fish

What do killer whales kill?

Killer whales are so fast and powerful that they can kill almost anything they wish—to eat, of course! Some killers form big, settled groups, called pods, that stay close to shore and eat mainly fish. Others live in smaller pods that travel more widely and hunt mostly sea mammals, such as whales, dolphins, seals, and sea lions.

Are killer whales smart?

Killer whales are among the most intelligent animals on Earth! They can remember where and when prey is plentiful each year. They also work together to surround and catch schools of fish, "talking" to each other using different noises, such as squeals and clicks.

Where do killer whales live?

Killer whales live in almost every sea and ocean around the world, with a total of about 50,000 living in the wild. They are most common in cool and cold waters and close to shore, and less common out in the middle of the open ocean and in warm, tropical regions.

SEA LIGHTS

Even on the brightest day, in the clearest sea, light soon fades with depth. Below 1,640 ft. (500 m), there is no sunlight at all. Yet there are strange glimmers and flashes all around because many sea animals can make their own glowing light, known as **bioluminescence**! They glow and shine to communicate with each other, camouflage their body, or lure prey.

BIOFLUORESCENCE, as shown by this anemone, is a neon glow in some animals. These animals absorb light and then give it off again as a different color. Biofluorescent animals are not able to turn their lights on and off like bioluminescent animals can.

anemone with clown fish

plankton

FAST FACT

Sometimes parts of the ocean can appear to twinkle. This is caused by types of bioluminescent **PLANKTON**. When the plankton sense movement, such as a wave or a boat, each one flashes—as a group, they twinkle!

FAST FACT

Sparkly **COMB JELLYFISH**, such as this sea walnut, are not bioluminescent. They have tiny cilia (moving hairs) that ripple along long bands that look like combs. The cilia reflect and scatter light, making the jellyfish sparkle!

sea walnut

dwarf lanternfish

FAST FACT

The bioluminescent **LANTERN FISH** has light-producing organs called photophores along its body. It glows to attract a mate and possibly to confuse predators by disguising its body shape.

BOTTOM 10

DEEP-SEA DWELLERS

The strangest creatures live at the bottom of the deepest oceans.

1 Slender hatchet fish

This fish has binocular vision, which means it can zoom in to view something far away—just like you can with a pair of binoculars!

Deep-sea anglerfish

Anglers have a head spine with a glowing tip to attract small fish and other prey—a little like a fishing rod!

Giant isopod

The giant isopod can grow to 28 in. (70 cm) long! It scavenges for pieces of food sinking from above.

Gulper or pelican eel

This fish is almost all mouth! Its jaws open wide so it can swallow prey bigger than itself.

Ratfish

A relative of sharks, this fish is also called a rabbitfish or chimaera. It has a venomous fin spine on its back.

Sea cucumber

The sea cucumber grows up to 3.3 ft. (1 m) long. It slides along the ocean floor, finding food in the mud and ooze.

Hadal snailfish

This fish is found over 26,250 ft. (8,000 m) deep! It may be called snailfish, but it has a tadpole-like tail.

Fang tooth

This fish has two fangs that are so long that its head needs sockets to fit them when its mouth is closed—a bit like a plug!

Dumbo octopus

This octopus has fin flaps that look like the ears of the cartoon elephant Dumbo. It lives up to 23,000 ft. (7,000 m) deep!

Bobtail squid

This squid has glowing bacteria in its mantle (body), to which it feeds a sugary fluid. The bacteria disguise it from predators!

Which deep-sea dweller is your number one?

OCEAN TREASURES

Seas and oceans provide many of our everyday needs—from important fuels to tasty fish sticks!

ISLAND PEOPLE catch fish, shellfish, and other foods. They aim to take enough for themselves and to sell locally, and leave the rest for the future.

* Half of Earth's **GAS** and **OIL** comes from under the sea. These fossil fuels are used to make plastics, paints, road surfaces, and hundreds of other products.

* Large numbers of **WIND TURBINES** in the sea are called wind farms. They turn the energy of moving air into electricity. Electricity is also made by tidal and wave power plants.

* Precious **METALS, MINERALS**, and **GEMS** come from mud and rocks under the sea. They include gold, silver, and even diamonds! They are scooped up by mechanical grabs or sucked up by enormous tubes.

* More than 90 percent of the products you buy in stores are **TRANSPORTED** by sea. From toys to cell phones, TVs to trucks—the list is endless!

* In some places, people use salt pans or artificial ponds full of seawater to farm the **SALT** you put in your food!

* **ARCHAEOLOGY** is the study of civilizations, buildings, art, and other remains, such as shipwrecks! There could be over three million shipwrecks on the ocean floor. Archaeology in the ocean is called "marine archaeology."

CLOSE UP

BEACH LIFE

Surfers love big, crashing waves, or "breakers," which can reach more than 65 ft. (20 m) tall in places such as Hawaii and Nazare, Portugal. When a wave makes a tunnel like this, surfers call it a "barrel" or "tube"—experienced surfers can surf inside a tube!

barrel

Surfing stats:

Highest wave surfed: 78 ft. (23.77 m)
Longest single surf: 3 hours, 55 min, 2 seconds (male)
Longest single surf: 2 hours, 18 min, 24 seconds (female)
Longest wave surfed by a dog: 351.7 ft. (107.2 m)

SAVE OUR SEAS!

The world's seas and oceans face many threats, and most are because of human activities. But we can all help by making small changes to our daily lives!

fishing trawler

GLOBAL WARMING

Earth's climate is changing because of human actions. Pollution causes the planet to get warmer—we call this global warming. Corals get their colors and much of their food from plantlike algae living in them. As the water grows warmer, the algae die and the coral loses its food and looks "bleached."

bleached coral

POLLUTION

Trash, such as glass or plastic bottles, floats in almost every ocean and sea. This is very dangerous for marine animals. Many creatures get tangled and cut in fishing nets. Turtles eat plastic bags because they look like their jellyfish food, and they soon die.

lionfish meets bag

oil pollution

OVERFISHING

Huge fishing boats scoop so many fish from the sea that there aren't enough fish to breed young for the future. The vast fishing nets can catch dolphins, seals, turtles, and other air breathers. The nets stop these animals from reaching the surface to breathe, so they drown.

trapped turtle

YOU CAN HELP!

You can answer the SOS! Here are some tips:

* When you're on the beach or swimming in the ocean, avoid damaging rocks, seaweeds, animals, and corals.

* Do not collect sea animals or plants. Leave them as part of the natural habitat.

* Do not buy souvenirs of dead animals, such as starfish and sea horses.

* Recycle plastic, glass, and other materials. This prevents them from getting into the sea, and saves natural resources taken from the sea.

* Save clean water when you can. This means less water is taken from seas, rivers, and lakes, and less energy is used to make it clean.

souvenir sea horse

TOP 10

WATER SPORTS!

There's always something to do by the ocean—or in it!

1 Flyboarding

Invented in 2012, the Flyboard is connected to a hose that spurts water or air down, shooting the Flyboard up at speeds reaching 93 mph (150 km/h)

2 Windsurfing

The windsurfer uses wind power to move. It can reach an incredible 52 knots—60 mph (96 km/h)!

3 Scuba diving

It is exciting to be part of the undersea world! "Scuba" means "**s**elf-**c**ontained **u**nderwater **b**reathing **a**pparatus."

4 Jet Skis

Water jets out of the back, making the Jet Ski race forward. Jet Skis can do amazing stunts!

5 Kitesurfing

More than two million kitesurfers belong to clubs worldwide. Experts can do more than 10 somersaults in midair!

6 Sailing

There are so many kinds of sailing craft, from small dinghies to huge, sleek ocean yachts. Sailing is an Olympic sport!

7 Paragliding

Beginner paragliders are towed by a boat, but experts steer wherever they wish—even landing on a moving boat!

8 Powerboats

The fastest powerboats roar along at more than 155 mph (250 km/h), which is twice the motorway speed limit!

9 Surfing

Island people have been surfing for centuries! It became popular in the 1900s, when the modern surfboard was invented.

10 Wakeboarders

Wakeboarders make amazing twists, turns, jumps, and loops while zipping along at more than 25 mph (40 km/h), towed behind a speedboat!

Which water sport is your number one?

THE OCEANS & SEAS QUIZ

Are you an expert on all things underwater? Test your knowledge by completing this quiz! When you've answered all of the questions, turn to page 63 to find your score.

 Which ocean is the smallest, shallowest, and coldest?
a) Arctic Ocean
b) Atlantic Ocean
c) Indian Ocean

 Which ocean current does the blue shark use to travel to reach Europe?
a) The Gelf Stream
b) The Golf Stream
c) The Gulf Stream

 The Mid-Atlantic Ridge is an . . .
a) Underwater mountain range
b) Underwater wall
c) Underwater volcano

 What is the Mariana Trench?
a) The coldest place on Earth
b) The deepest place on Earth
c) The highest place on Earth

 How many seas are there on Earth?
a) Fewer than 50
b) Fewer than 90
c) More than 100

 Mangroves grow on shores where . . .
a) Currents are gentle
b) Currents are moderate
c) Currents are strong

When an animal's colors and shape blend in with its surroundings, we call it . . .
a) Camouflaged
b) Cornered
c) Covered up

 What percentage of Earth's ocean animals live in coral reefs?
a) 10 percent
b) 15 percent
c) 25 percent

 Which bird has the longest wings of all?
a) Albatross
b) Pelican
c) Puffin

Which ocean creature is the biggest animal on Earth?
a) Whale shark
b) Blue whale
c) Great white shark

 What is blubber?
a) A jellylike layer of fat
b) A thick layer of fur
c) A smooth layer of scales

 How long can Greenland sleeper sharks live for?
a) Fewer than 50 years
b) About 150 years
c) More than 350 years

 How warm is a penguin under its feathers?
a) 77°F (25°C)
b) 89.6°F (32°C)
c) 100.4°F (38°C)

 What is the name for a group of dolphins?
a) A pad
b) A pod
c) A putt

 How many shark attacks are there each year?
a) 10–50
b) 50–100
c) 100–1,000

 Where do female loggerhead turtles lay their eggs?
a) In a coral reef
b) Near rocky cliffs
c) On the beach where they hatched

 Which animal is sometimes called an orca or blackfish?
a) Common dolphin
b) Killer whale
c) Sperm whale

 What was the longest wave surfed by a dog?
a) 32.8 ft. (10 m)
b) 180.5 ft. (55 m)
c) 351.7 ft. (107.2 m)

 Which of these sports is an Olympic sport?
a) Flyboarding
b) Sailing
c) Scuba diving

 Which ocean covers about one-third of Earth's surface?
a) The Atlantic Ocean
b) The Indian Ocean
c) The Pacific Ocean

GLOSSARY

bar
A long, low, narrow mound, usually made of sand, that may be underwater at high tide. Generally, both ends are attached to the land.

bioluminescence
Light produced by living things. Many ocean animals are bioluminescent, as are glowworms and fireflies on land.

blubber
A thick layer of fat under the skin of many polar and ocean creatures, that helps keep them warm.

breeding
When a male and a female animal come together to produce young.

camouflage
The colors and patterns of an animal that help it blend in with its surroundings. This disguise helps it hide from predators or creep up on prey without being seen.

earthquake
A violent shaking felt on the Earth's surface, caused by sudden movements of its continents.

fissure
A narrow, deep, steep-sided crack or crevice.

gravity
The force that attracts objects toward each other. The greater an object's mass, the greater its pull of gravity. Earth's tides are caused mainly by the Moon's gravity, and also the Sun's.

hurricane
A huge storm, hundreds of miles across, with swirling winds faster than 74 mph (120 km/h), and massive amounts of rain.

spit

A long, low narrow mound, usually of sand or shingle. A spit that sticks out into the water, generally with one end attached to the land.

tornado

A tall, moving, funnel-shaped area of fast-spinning winds, usually beneath large storm clouds.

tropics

The areas around the middle of Earth, about 1,616 mi. (2,600 km) on each side of the equator. They are usually warm all year round.

lava

Hot, molten rock that erupts onto the surface of a planet and starts to flow.

low tide mark

The farthest point down the shore that the sea reaches at low tide. Below this mark is underwater all the time.

mountain range

A long row or chain of high peaks, on land or underwater.

seamount

A mountain that rises from the sea-bed, but its top or peak is underwater, not above the surface.

shallows

An area of water that is not very deep. Coral reefs are usually found in the shallows.

shingle

Loose pebble and cobble stones, mostly up to about 8 in. (20 cm) across, usually rounded by being rubbed together.

skeleton

The strong supporting framework of a living thing. Fish, amphibians, reptiles, birds, and mammals have an inner skeleton of bones.

QUIZ ANSWERS: 1 = a, 2 = c, 3 = a, 4 = b, 5 = c, 6 = a, 7 = a, 8 = c, 9 = a, 10 = b, 11 = a, 12 = c, 13 = c, 14 = b, 15 = b, 16 = c, 17 = b, 18 = c, 19 = b, 20 = c.

INDEX